ADAM ROSE ■ CHARLES TOEFIELD

For Markosia Enterprises Ltd

Harry Markos
Publisher & Managing Partner

GM Jordan
Special Projects Co-ordinator

Annika Eade
Media Manager

Andy Briggs
Creative Consultant

Meiron Jones
Marketing Director

Ian Sharman
Editor In Chief

Playground™ & © 2017 Adam Rose & Markosia Enterprises, Ltd. All Rights Reserved. Reproduction of any part of this work by any means without the written permission of the publisher is expressly forbidden. All names, characters and events in this publication are entirely fictional. Any resemblance to actual persons, living or dead is purely coincidental. Published by Markosia Enterprises, PO BOX 3477, Barnet, Hertfordshire, EN5 9HN. FIRST PRINTING, December 2017. Harry Markos, Director.

ISBN 978-1-911243-57-1

www.markosia.com

PLAYGROUND FOREWORD

The sidewalk was always lava.

If you were playing any kind of game at recess that involved imagination and role-playing, and it involved some sort of arbitrary boundary, the sidewalk, somehow, was always lava. You stepped on it, you were "dead." Other made-up boundaries could be alligator pits, cliffs, force fields, or the ocean, but the sidewalk... It was a universal truth of childhood: The sidewalk was always lava.

It didn't matter what kind of game you were playing. In my case, if Mario, Mike, Scott, Bryan, Ryan, Mansa, Lee and I were setting off on some mission behind enemy lines in the waning days of World War II, if we were rocketing into the cold wastes of outerspace to bring back captured humans from a sinister alien race, ifwe were shooting it out with Capone's thugs on the streets of 1920s Chicago... The sidewalk was always lava. Maybe it's written into the genetic code somehow. Or our parents whisper it to us in our cribs. Or our schools infect us with the notion by way of some additive to our cafeteria lunches for reasons still unknown. But it was a constant. An un-questioned, unchallenged, simply accepted constant. Around which everything else changed every time you stepped onto that black canvas called the playground.

Playgrounds are dense forests of imagination. It's amazing anyone can cross from one side to the other with the wild, brilliant, intricate ideas whizzing around. That's not a sandbox, it's an archeological dig. That's not a jungle gym, it's a spaceship. And those swings? They're catapults for fending off the barbarians at our gates. The playground is where anything can happen if you just dream hard enough.

With this darkly whimsical new graphic novel, Adam Rose and Charles Toefield have perfectly captured that spirit of wonder, excitement, and unpredictability. Except on their *Playground*, some of the things we only dreamed during our breaks between classes are hilariously, scarily, thrillingly real. The rules reveal themselves on every new page. Only Adam and Charles know where they're taking us, and we're happy to hang on for dear life and let them. The best part is that the bell isn't going to ring and pull you away if you don't want to go. *Playground* is a great ride and I'm jealous that you're just starting out on it.

Just don't step on the sidewalk.

-Adam Beechen
Los Angeles, 2015

Adam Beechen is a comic book writer and animation writer. He is the producer and writer on the 2015 *Transformers: Robots in Disguise* cartoon. In the field of comics, he has written primarily for D.C. Comics, on *Countdown to Final Crisis*, *Justice League Unlimited*, *Batman*, related titles of various stripes, and *Teen Titans*. In animation, he's written for many shows including *Littlest Pet Shop*, *Scooby Doo! Mystery Incorporated*, and *Jackie Chan Adventures*, and story edited on *Hi Hi Puff AmiYumi*, *Pink Panther & Pals*, and *Edgar & Ellen*.

TABLE OF CONTENTS

FELIX'S EMBLEMS

PLAYGROUND: ATTACK OF THE GURGLE BOTS

DOUBLE FEATURE: CHECKMATE
                PLAYGROUND

HOBBY SQUAD

COLOR FUN COLORING PAGES

MAKE-YOUR-OWN EMBLEM

ADDITIONAL ARTWORK

ARTIST BIOS AND ACKNOWLEDGEMENTS

PLAYGROUND AND ALL BACK UP STORIES
CREATED BY ADAM ROSE

PLAYGROUND: ATTACK OF THE GURGLE BOTS
ILLUSTRATED BY CHARLES TOEFIELD

COVER ART: CHARLES TOEFIELD

LETTERER AND COLORIST: SHAUNA KLEBESADEL

PLAYGROUND ADDITIONAL SHORT ILLUSTRATED,
COLORED AND LETTERED BY DAVID PENTLAND

PLAYGROUND "CHECKMATE" BACKUP ILLUSTRATED,
COLORED AND LETTERED BY TREVOR A. SMITH

HOBBY SQUAD ILLUSTRATED, LETTERED AND
COLORED BY SHAUNA KLEBESADEL

FELIX'S

FREEZE TAG

WHEN FELIX SAYS THE NAME OF A CHILDHOOD GAME OUT-LOUD, HE CHANNELS THE POWER OF THAT GAME. SO, WHEN HE YELLS "FREEZE TAG!" HE CAN TOUCH ANYONE NEAR HIM, AND THEY WILL LITERALLY FREEZE.

THE PERSON HE TOUCHES BECOMES COVERED IN A THIN LAYER OF ICE, AND STAYS FROZEN UNTIL SOMEONE ELSE "UNFREEZES" THEM BY TOUCHING THE PERSON.

TUNNEL TAG

IF FELIX IS FACING OFF WITH SOMEONE AND NEEDS TO ESCAPE, HE YELLS, "TUNNEL TAG!" WHEN TUNNEL TAG IS DECLARED, A PERFECT TUNNEL IS CREATED RIGHT AT HIS FEET AND OPENS UP ON THE OTHER SIDE OF WHATEVER OBSTACLE HE'S FACING.

THE TUNNEL CLOSES AS IF IT WERE NEVER THERE ONCE HE IS THROUGH IT.

TV TAG

DURING A GAME OF TV TAG, IF FELIX TAKES A KNEE AND FORMS A "T" WITH HIS HANDS, HE BECOMES WHATEVER TELEVISION SHOW HE SAYS.

ONCE 30 SECONDS ARE UP, HE RETURNS TO NORMAL, AND THEN MUST THINK OF SOME OTHER TV SHOW TO BECOME SOMETHING NEW. ONCE HE'S USED A SHOW, HE CAN NEVER USE IT AGAIN.

HIDE AND SEEK

THIS POWER WORKS IN TWO WAYS. IF SOMEONE IS HIDING FROM FELIX AND HE YELLS "OLLY OLLY OXIN FREE!" THEN THAT PERSON'S POSITION IS REVEALED.

IF FELIX NEEDS TO HIDE AND HE YELLS "HIDE AND SEEK" THEN HE BLENDS INTO WHATEVER BACKGROUND IS IN FOR TWENTY SECONDS-- AS LONG AS HE IS PERFECTLY STILL.

EMBLEMS

MOTHER MAY I
IMBUES THREE POWERS TO FELIX:

1) SHOUTING "GIANT LEAP" LETS HIM LEAP OVER A MAXIMUM OF A 5-STORY BUILDING.

2) SHOUTING "BABY STEP" WILL ALLOW HIM TO GINGERLY WALK THROUGH AN ALARM SYSTEM, MINE FIELD, ETC, WITHOUT SETTING ANYTHING OFF.

3) SHOUTING "LEAP FROG" AND BOOM! THE PARTICIPANT BECOMES A HUMAN-SIZED FROG. WATCH OUT FOR **FLIES**...

RED-LIGHT-GREEN-LIGHT
IF FELIX YELLS "RED LIGHT," EVERYONE AROUND HIM IS BATHED IN A RED GLOW AND FROZEN IN PLACE UNTIL HE YELLS "GREEN LIGHT." STRICT IS IMMUNE, THANKS TO HIS OWN SUGAR BASED ABILITIES.

SIMON SAYS

IF FELIX SAYS "SIMON SAYS" AND GIVES SOME SIMPLE INSTRUCTION, THE PERSON IS COMPELLED TO DO WHATEVER "SIMON SAYS." IF THEY DON'T, THEY ARE "OUT," AND BEING "OUT" KNOCKS A PERSON UNCONCIOUS FOR 5 MINUTES.

DUCK, DUCK, GOOSE!
A LIFESAVING GAME FOR FELIX! IF HE IS IN THE DUCK-DUCK-GOOSE CIRCLE AND SOMEONE IS SMART ENOUGH (MELINDA) TO TAP HIS HEAD AND CALL OUT ANY ANIMAL (LIKE A LION...) FELIX TEMPORARILY TRANSFORMS INTO THAT ANIMAL.

STRICT.

PRINCIPAL STRICT AKA **AGENT STRICT** HAS THE ABILITY TO DISH OUT ICE CREAM HEADACHES, TOO-MUCH-CANDY TUMMY ACHES, AND MANIPULATE ALL FORMS OF CANDY TO DO HIS BIDDING.

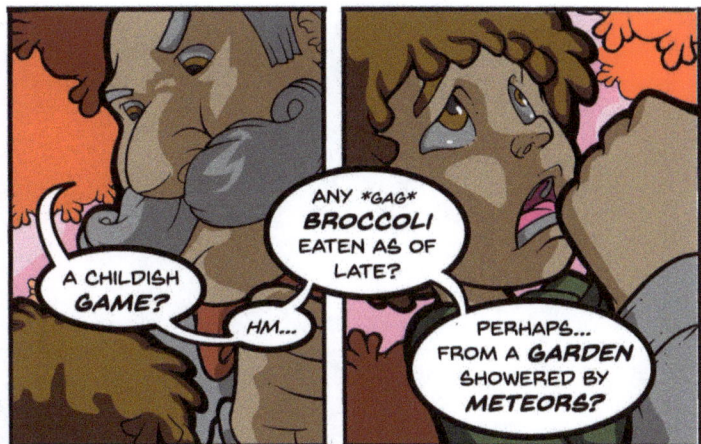

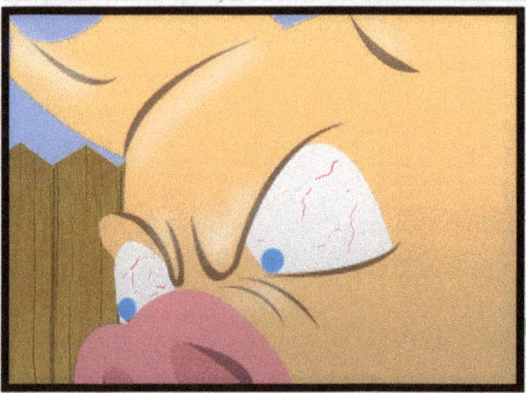

COLOR FUN!

**YOU'VE SEEN THE GURGLE BOTS IN ACTION!
NOW IT'S YOUR TURN TO COLOR 'EM IN!**

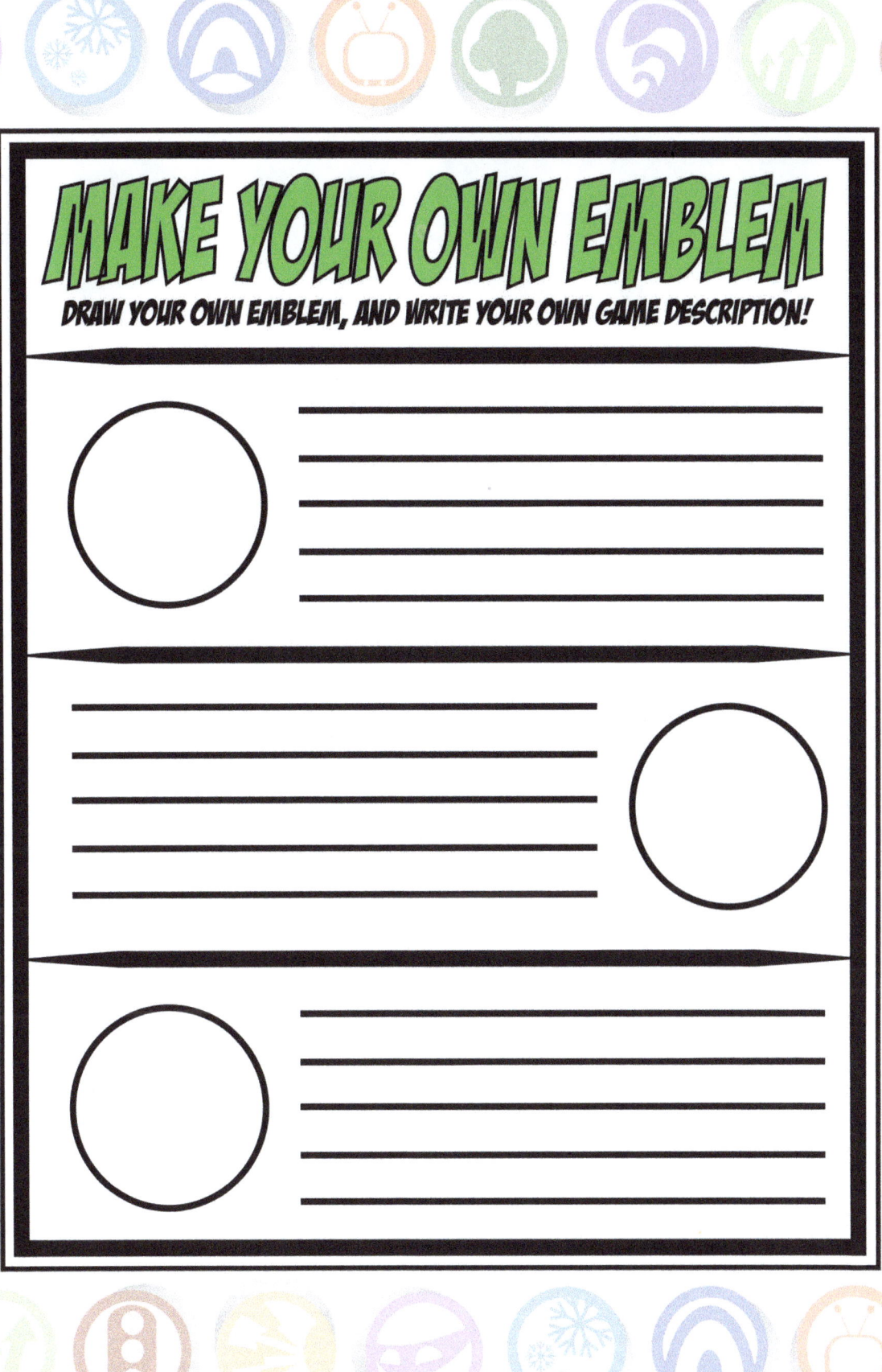

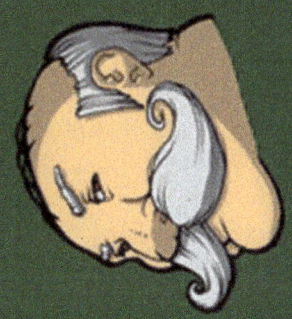

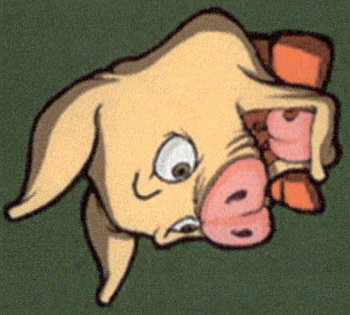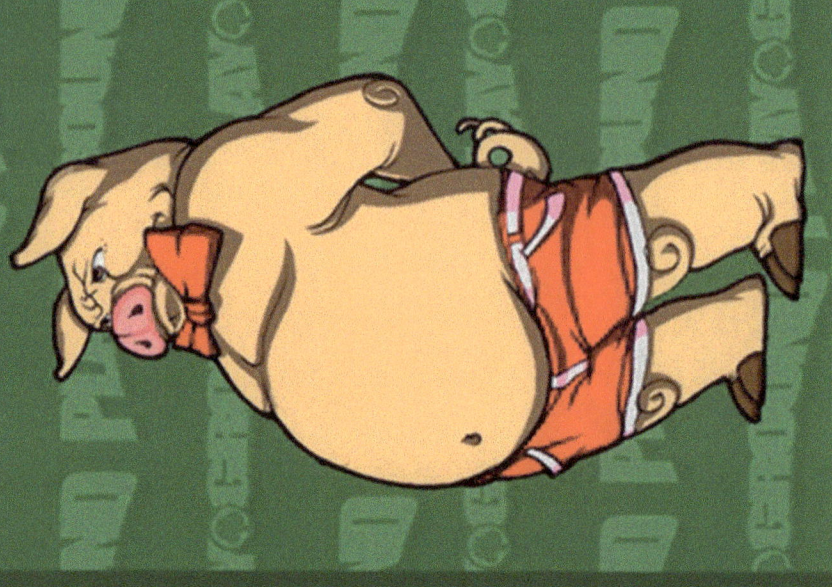

PLAYGROUND

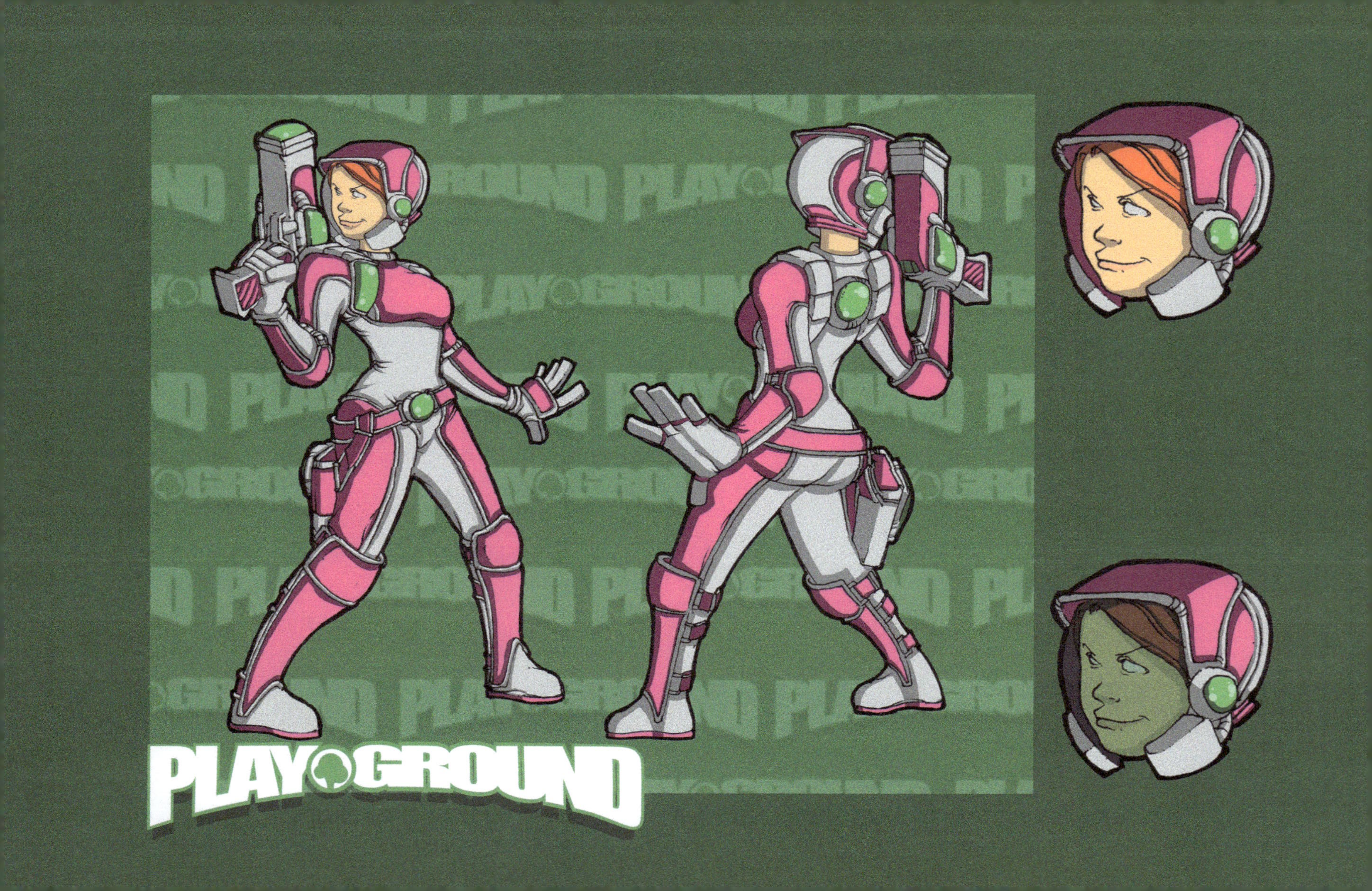

PLAYGROUND

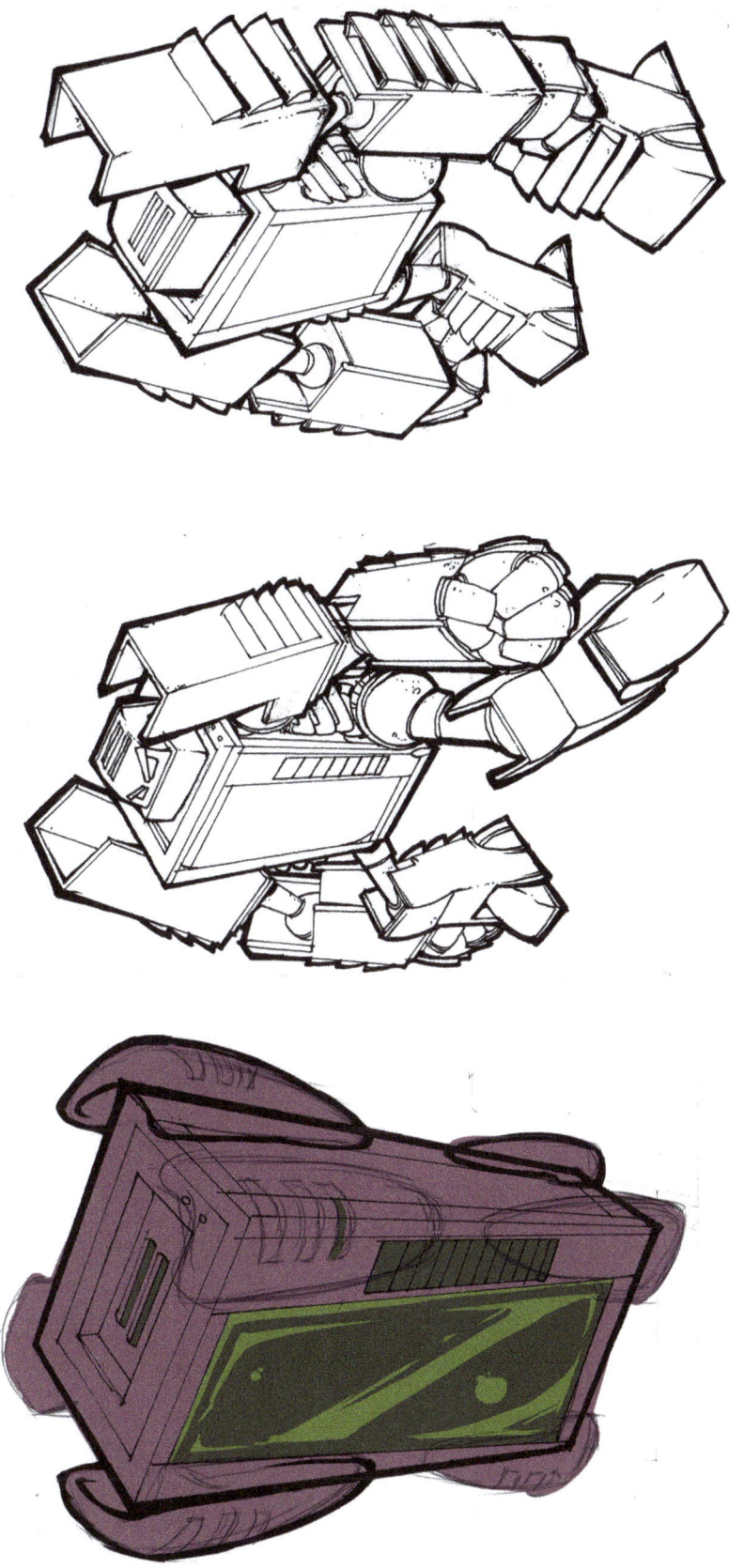

Additional character art by Nate Healey

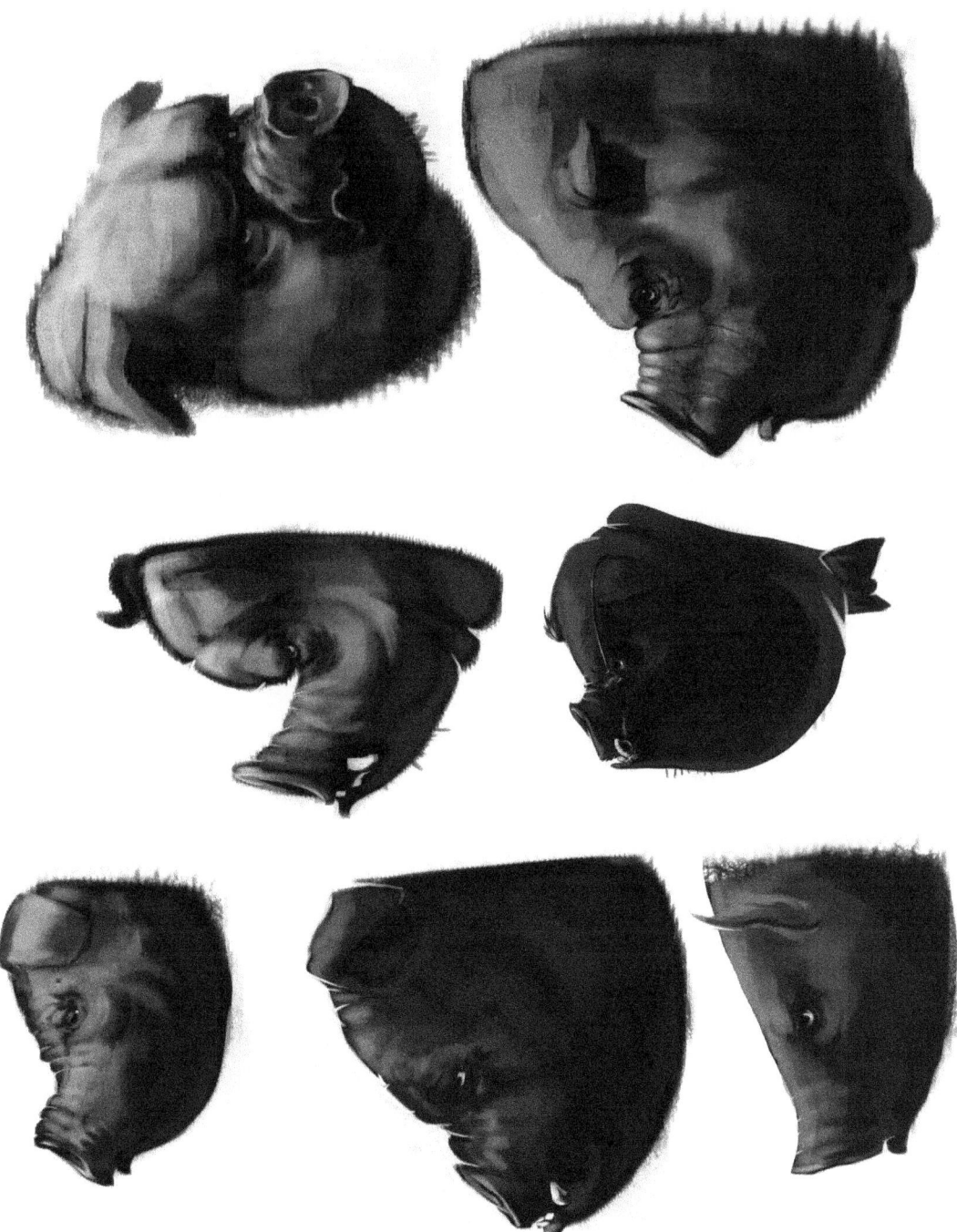

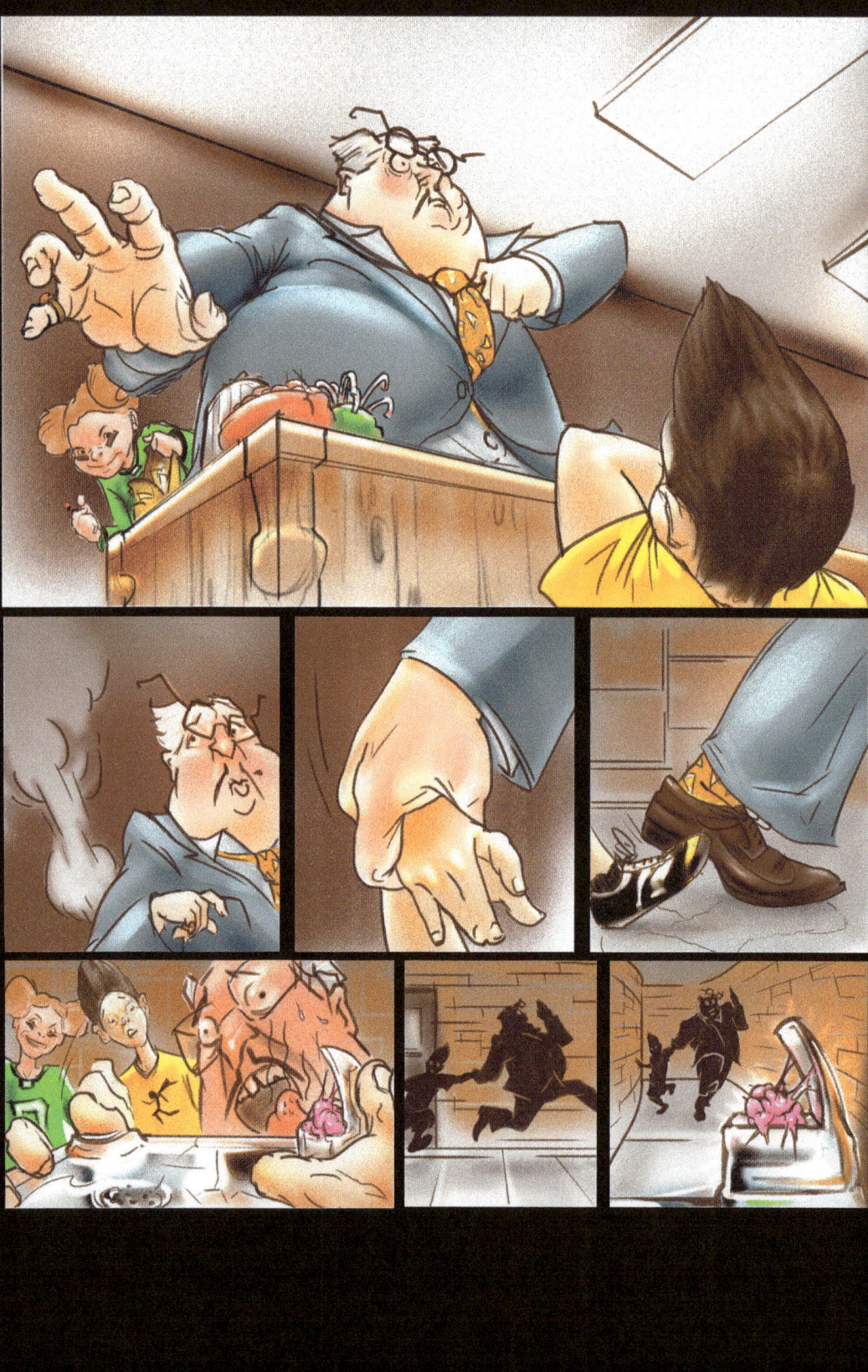

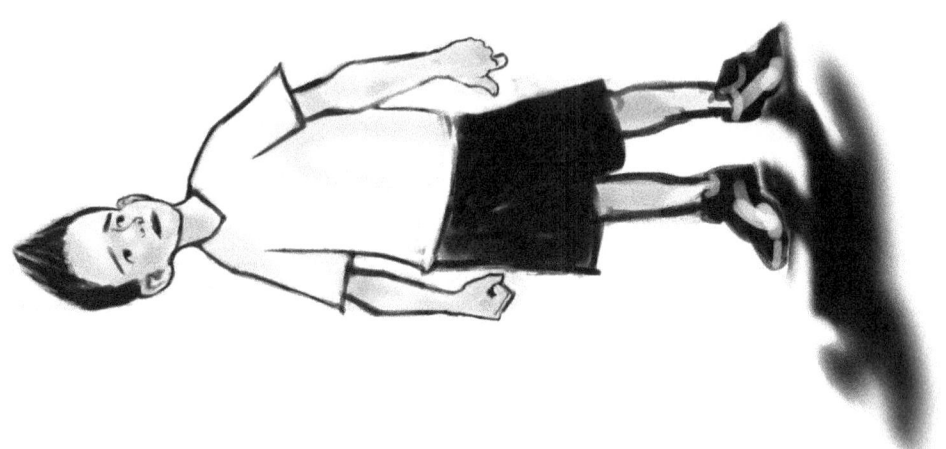

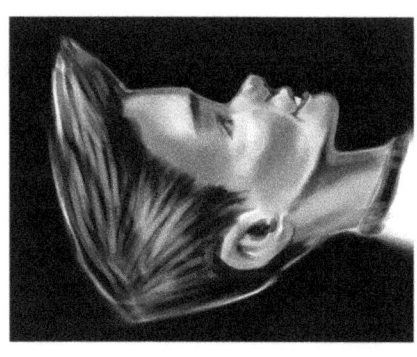 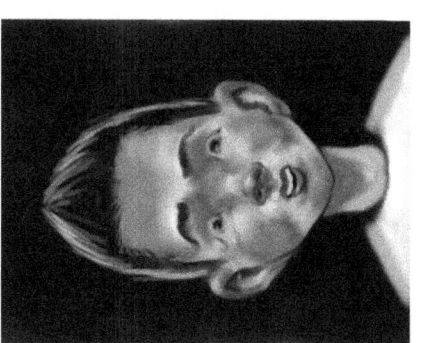

BIOS

Adam Rose is a writer and TV tag enthusiast living in Los Angeles. He hopes kids read Playground, put down their electronic gizmos, and discover some of his favorite childhood games. If they have any other games they'd like to see Felix Tremendez aka PLAYGROUND use as a super power, email him at: adamsupermallman@gmail.com.

Charles Toefield is a Maryland based Illustrator working in the areas of Comic Art, Children's Illustration, and Character Design. Charles was originally born in the Maryland area and entered the professional illustration industry in 2010. Charles currently lives with his wife, child, three dogs and a mischievous black cat affectionately named Yodah.

Shauna Klebesadel currently studies at Gnomon with a concentration in 3D Modeling and Texturing after earning her English degree from UCLA in 2013. As a game and comic enthusiast, she was thrilled to participate in the fun and the many creative possibilities of this playful story.

David Pentland is a Los Angeles based artist studying design for entertainment.

Trevor A. Smith was born in 1985 and raised in Echo Park, CA. He resides with his wife and many kitties on their spacecraft "Perseverance." When he is not seeking adventure on the Space-ways, he can be found drawing, metal/wood working, and enjoying the "Human" sport of eating BBQ ribs.

ACKNOWLEDGEMENTS

Playground and all its parts have been quite the labor of love, and I couldn't have done it without the support of my wife and two playground trekking kids: Sigrid, Felix and Karoline.
I also want to thank my mom and dad: Howard and Kathy Rose for all their love, support, and encouragement.

Thanks, as well, to my great team of artists.

Originally Playground was set to have a slightly different look and feel. Artist, Nate Healy, came up some of the earliest character designs, and one almost finished page.

Charles started the whole process with his final versions of character designs. Felix's hair changed a bit during the process but everyone else stayed the same.

David came into the process later in the game but I am psyched to have had him involved! The mini back up story I wrote for him has a bit of a Bazooka Joe/ old Archie vibe, and he nailed it with the pacing!

Shauna rocked out on the lettering and final coloring of almost every part of this book. She also really got to shine with the whole Hobby Squad backup story!

~ Adam Rose

www.ingramcontent.com/pod-product-compliance
Lightning Source LLC
LaVergne TN
LVHW070948070426
835507LV00028B/3451